SEA AND SKY
MONSTERS

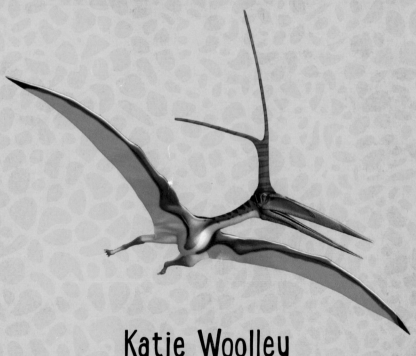

Katie Woolley

Published in paperback in Great Britain in 2018
by Wayland

Copyright © Hodder and Stoughton 2018

Editor: Elise Short

Design: Peter Clayman

Illustrations: Martin Bustamante

ISBN: 978 1 5263 0466 7

MIX
Paper from
responsible sources
FSC
www.fsc.org   FSC® C104740

10 9 8 7 6 5 4 3 2 1

Wayland, an imprint of
Hachette Children's Group
Part of Hodder and Stoughton
Carmelite House
50 Victoria Embankment
London EC4Y 0DZ

An Hachette UK Company
www.hachette.co.uk
www.hachettechildrens.co.uk

Printed and bound in China

Picture acknowledgements:
All images courtesy of Shutterstock except
p8-9 iStock: MR1805; cover image; p17 tr; p18-
9; p22-23; p26-27, p28-29: illustrated by Martin
Bustamante

CONTENTS

PREHISTORIC NEIGHBOURS

Dinosaurs roamed the Earth, during the **Mesozoic Era** (251–65 million years ago). But they weren't the only **creatures** that lived during this era and beyond.

Giant reptiles soared high in the sky and **marine monsters** swam in the seas and oceans, too.

This flying creature is **Dimorphodon**, pronounced DIE-more-foh-don. Its name means two-formed tooth, because it had two kinds of teeth.

Most plesiosaurs had **long necks** to help them **strike out** and **catch their prey**.

Plesiosaurs [PLEE-see-oh-sore] were **meat-eating marine reptiles**. They used their **flippers** to move through the water.

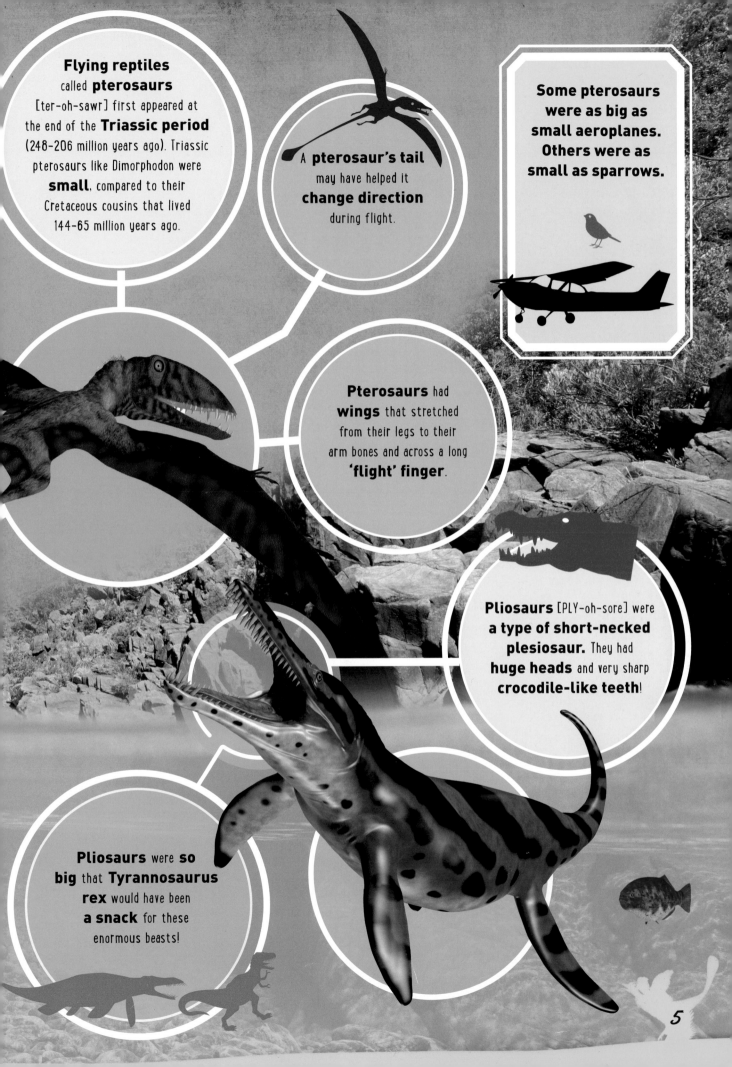

Flying reptiles called **pterosaurs** [ter-oh-sawr] first appeared at the end of the **Triassic period** (248-206 million years ago). Triassic pterosaurs like Dimorphodon were **small**, compared to their Cretaceous cousins that lived 144-65 million years ago.

A **pterosaur's tail** may have helped it **change direction** during flight.

Some pterosaurs were as big as small aeroplanes. Others were as small as sparrows.

Pterosaurs had **wings** that stretched from their legs to their arm bones and across a long **'flight' finger**.

Pliosaurs [PLY-oh-sore] were **a type of short-necked plesiosaur.** They had **huge heads** and very sharp **crocodile-like teeth**!

Pliosaurs were **so big** that **Tyrannosaurus rex** would have been **a snack** for these enormous beasts!

MONSTERS OF THE SEA

Dinosaurs may have ruled the land, but the **prehistoric monsters of the sea** were not dinosaurs. They were **fierce aquatic reptiles**, which lurked in the watery depths below.

Liopleurodon, pronounced LIE-oh-PLOOR-oh-don, means smooth-sided teeth.

FOOD → CHAIN

Liopleurodon was an **enormous pliosaur** with huge teeth. At **45 cm**, each **tooth** was twice the size of a Tyrannosaurus rex's.

Liopleurodon may have grown to 25 m. That's as long as a blue whale!

Prehistoric sea creatures were part of a **food chain**, just like the dinosaurs on land. **Squid** would have been **eaten by reptiles** like ichthyosaurs. They, in turn, would have been a **tasty lunch for larger reptiles** such as Liopleurodon.

Ichthyosaurs were **giant reptiles** that lived during the Jurassic period (206-144 million years ago). They are often called '**sea dragons**'.

At **21 m long**, **Shastasaurus** [shass-tah-SORE-us] is the **biggest-known ichthyosaur**. It didn't have any teeth but may have sucked its prey into its mouth.

ichthyosaur
[IK-thee-oh-SORE]

Ichthyosaurs had **large eyes. Temnodontosaurus** [tem-NO-don-tuh-SORE-us] had eyes **as big as dinner plates**. It probably dived into the dark sea depths looking for food.

squid

Ichthyosaurs used their **speed** to quickly dart away from **predators**, such as Liopleurodon.

It's been said that the **Loch Ness Monster** is a **plesiosaur** that got **trapped in the loch** when the sea retreated millions of years ago.

INCREDIBLE ICHTHYOSAURS

The most famous ichthyosaur is **Ichthyosaurus**. It may have looked like a **dolphin** but this **prehistoric reptile** was, in fact, a distant relative of lizards and snakes. It lived during the **Late Triassic** (237–206 million years ago) and **Early Jurassic periods** (206–174 million years ago).

Ichthyosaurus, pronounced ICK-thee-oh-SORE-us, means fish lizard.

Ichthyosaurus had **four fins** on the sides of its body and a dorsal (back) fin to keep it stable in the water. It moved its **fish-like tail fin** from side to side to **propel** itself through the water.

Ichthyosaurus was one of the smallest ichthyosaurs. It was still **2 m long**. That's as long as a **giant stingray** is wide.

Fossil remains of smaller Ichthyosauruses have been **found inside** bigger ones. Scientists think Ichthyosaurus gave **birth** to **live young**. They may have been **born tail first**.

Its **streamlined body** helped Ichthyosaurus move swiftly through the water. It could swim at **34 kilometres per hour** (kph). That's about the **same speed as a dolphin**.

Ichthyosaurus had **large eyes** that were close together to help it **spot its prey**.

Ichthyosaurus could not breathe underwater. It had to swim to the surface to breathe in air through **nostrils** close to its eyes, on top of its snout.

Another ichthyosaur, **Eurhinosaurus** [you-RINE-oh-SORE-us] looked like a **modern swordfish**. It is thought that it used its 'sword' to slash through shoals of small fish.

Ichthyosaurus used its **sharp teeth** and **long snout** to catch fish and squid.

POWERFUL PLESIOSAURS AND PLIOSAURS

Plesiosaurs first appeared in the **Late Triassic era** and lived through the rest of the **Mesozoic Era**. These **enormous meat-eaters** feasted on huge amounts of fish, squid and molluscs!

Elasmosaurus was **14 m long**. Its **neck** was **7 m**, half its full length. A giraffe's neck is only 1.8 m!

This plesiosaur is an **Elasmosaurus**, pronounced el-AZ-moh-sore-us. Its name means thin-plated lizard.

Some **plesiosaurs swallowed stones** that acted as **weights to help them sink** to the ocean floor in search of food.

Plesiosaurs had big front **flippers** and smaller back flippers. They used them to **swim in the same way turtles do today**.

Plesiosaurs had **long pointed teeth** for capturing rather than chewing their prey. They probably **swallowed their food whole!**

These marine reptiles lived in the oceans but they couldn't breathe underwater. They **needed to go to the surface for air.**

Plesiosaurs had long necks, small heads and wide bodies.

Liopleurodon, a pliosaur (see p 6), was a huge **aquatic predator** but it didn't have speed on its side. It **swam at about 10 kph.** That's about the **same as an otter.** Its jaws were longer than a canoe.

Pliosaurs were a type of plesiosaur. They had **large heads** with **strong jaws** and **short necks**.

This pliosaur is a **Kronosaurus,** pronounced CROW-noh-SORE-us.

Pliosaurs had bigger back flippers than front ones.

At **11 m long,** Kronosaurus was **bigger than a killer whale!**

Pliosaurs ate plesiosaurs!
A fossil of Elasmosaurus was found with bite marks from the giant pliosaur Kronosaurus.

By the end of the **Cretaceous period,** plesiosaurs and pliosaurs had had to **make way** for the mighty **mosasaurs** (see pages 12-13).

MIGHTY MOSASAURS

The mosasaurs [MO-zah-sore] were the rulers of the waves during the **Late Cretaceous period**. Fossils have been found on almost every continent of the world, so mosasaurs were as widespread in the water as the dinosaurs were on land!

This mosasaur is a **Tylosaurus**, pronounced TIE-loh-sore-us. Its name means knob lizard.

Mosasaurs moved the back of their body and their **long tail** from side to side to **propel** themselves through the water.

Hainosaurus
[HIGH-no-SORE-us] was a mosasaur that grew to about **12 m long** - about the **length of a humpback whale**.

Mosasaurs could expand their jaws to eat their prey whole, like a snake.

Most mosasaurs had **fish, plesiosaurs, turtles, ammonites** and other **mosasaurs** for their **lunch**.

Mosasaurs had **one enemy** – prehistoric **sharks**! One fossil has the marks of a shark's teeth in its spine.

Tylosaurus used its **snout** when **attacking prey** rather than its teeth. It would **ram** it with such force that its prey would be stunned.

Globidens
[Glo-bih-denz] was a mosasaur with **rounded teeth**. It used its teeth to **crush prey** such as **turtles and shellfish**.

A **Hainosaurus fossil** has been found with part of a **giant turtle** in its stomach!

Mosasaurs became **extinct** at the **same time as the last of the dinosaurs**, around **65 million years ago**.

MEGA MEGALODON

Megalodon was an enormous **prehistoric shark** that is possibly the most **fearsome predator** to have ever lived. It roamed the seas between 23 million years ago and 2.6 million years ago, after the age of the dinosaurs.

The height of Megalodon's **tail fin** alone was **4 m**. That's about the **same length as a male great white shark**.

Megalodon, pronounced MEG-ah-low-don, means big tooth.

Megalodons lived **in all oceans of the world**. They **hunted** in the **open sea** and may have **rushed from below**, taking their prey by surprise.

This mighty creature **weighed** about 60,000 kg. That's more than **70 giant squids!**

Megalodon ate **giant turtles, whales** and **mammals** such as Odobenocetops [oh-doh-ben-OH-set-ops].

Megalodon possibly **tore off the fins of large prey** first so it couldn't swim away.

In **one bite** of its **gigantic jaws**, Megalodon could have **crushed a car** with a force up to **30 times stronger than that of a lion**.

Its jaws were home to 276 giant teeth in six rows.

Megalodon's **fossilised teeth** were once **mistaken for dragon tongues**. Each one was **17 cm long** - about the length of a banana.

Megalodon was about **18 m long**. That's as long as **three great white sharks**.

THE BIG, THE BAD AND THE UGLY

Prehistoric seas were full of weird and wonderful creatures, just like the oceans today. Here are some of the prehistoric creatures that once lived beneath the waves ...

ARCHELON

PRONUNCIATION: ARK-eh-lon

TYPE: Reptile

SIZE: 4.6 m

LIVED: Late Cretaceous

PREDATORS: Mosasaurs and sharks

FACT: This turtle was twice as big as the largest turtle today – the leatherback.

CRASSIGYRINUS

PRONUNCIATION: CRASS-ee-jih-RYE-nuss

TYPE: Early amphibian

SIZE: Up to 2 m long

LIVED: 359-323 million years ago

PREDATORS: Unknown

FACT: Crassigyrinus had unusually large jaws, which had two rows of sharp teeth, including a pair of fangs in the second row. It probably swallowed its prey whole.

DUNKLEOSTEUS

PRONUNCIATION: dunk-lee-OWE-stee-us

TYPE: Fish

SIZE: 8-10 m long

LIVED: 370-360 million years ago

PREDATORS: None

FACT: For such a fierce predator, it didn't have any teeth. Dunkleosteus used bony plates with sharp points to bite through its prey.

STETHACANTHUS

PRONUNCIATION: STETH-ac-anth-us

TYPE: Fish

SIZE: 0.7-2 m long

LIVED: 370-345 million years ago

PREDATORS: Dunkleosteus

FACT: Surfs up! Stethacanthus was a shark with a dorsal fin shaped like a surfboard. It would have had no problem recognising others of its own species.

LEEDSICHTHYS

PRONUNCIATION: Leeds-ICK-thees

TYPE: Fish

SIZE: Up to 27 m long

LIVED: Late Jurassic

PREDATORS: Liopleurodon

FACT: Possibly the largest fish ever to have lived. It had 40,000 teeth that filtered the water to pick out tiny shrimp, jellyfish and small fish.

PTERYGOTUS

PRONUNCIATION: terry-GO-tuss

TYPE: Giant sea scorpion

SIZE: Up to 2.3 m long

LIVED: 444-389 million years ago

PREDATORS: Armoured fish such as Dunkleosteus

FACT: Fossils of Pterygotus have been found on every continent except Antarctica.

EARLY MONSTERS OF THE SKIES

Dinosaurs probably didn't fly but the skies weren't empty during the **Mesozoic Era**. **Flying reptiles**, called **pterosaurs**, flew above the Earth. They first appeared during the **Triassic period**.

This flying creature is an **Austriadactylus** pronounced OSS-tree-ah-dak-tyl-us. Its name means Austria finger.

Triassic pterosaurs were the **first animals to fly**, apart from insects. Their **wings** were made of **skin**, **muscles** and other **body tissues**.

Early pterosaurs were small, with long, narrow tails and wings.

Most pterosaurs lived near water and ate fish and shellfish. Some species lived further in land. They probably **ate young dinosaurs, eggs, insects and other animals**.

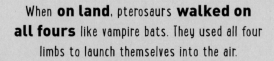

When **on land**, pterosaurs **walked on all fours** like vampire bats. They used all four limbs to launch themselves into the air.

Pterosaurs had **hollow bones**. This meant they could get **up into the air** easily – although **bigger pterosaurs** needed a bit of **a run up!**

 Some pterosaurs could **fly** at **speeds of 120 kph** – that's **as fast as a running cheetah!**

Many pterosaurs sported **head crests**. The crests may have been used to **attract a mate** or to **get rid of heat as they flew**.

Young pterosaurs could probably survive on their own as soon as they hatched. Their wings helped them get into the air and away from predators as quickly as possible.

pterosaur wing

Their **large wings** were supported in the air by an **extra long fourth finger**.

Eudimorphodon [you-DIE-mor-fo-don] was an early pterosaur from the Triassic period. It had **100 teeth** in its long jaws!

Later Cretaceous pterosaurs grew to enormous sizes. Some may have lived in large **flocks**, hunting on foot **like herons.**

Pterosaurs disappeared from Earth along with the dinosaurs 65 million years ago.

IMPRESSIVE PTERANODON

Pteranodon was a flying reptile that existed during the **Late Cretaceous period**, about 75 million years ago. This massive creature lived near the **coast of North America** and probably had a **diet of fish and squid**.

Pteranodon, pronounced teh-RAN-oh-don, means no teeth.

Like many Cretaceous pterosaurs, Pteranodon had a **short tail**, **big wings** and a **large head**.

Pteranodon spent most of its days **flying** over the **sea** and hardly any time on land.

Its **wing shape** meant it could **fly much like an eagle**, soaring over huge distances in its search for food.

Pteranodon's large brain and excellent eyesight made it a clever hunter.

Pteranodon had a large **pointed crest** on its head. It may have used the crest **to stabilise its flight, like the rudder on a boat**.

Pteranodon looked a bit like a **giant pelican**. It was **as tall as a man**, with a **long jaw and beak**!

Pteranodon didn't have any teeth! Its beak was toothless, just like a bird. It probably **scooped up its food** as it flew low over the water.

Its wingspan was 6 m across. That's as wide as a three-storey building is tall.

HUGE HATZEGOPTERYX

Hatzegopteryx is one of the **largest flying animals** to have ever lived. Its home was Hateg Island, near modern-day Romania. This pterosaur was **over 5 m tall** and hunted both in the air and on land.

Hatzegopteryx, pronounced HAT-zeh-GOP-teh-rix, means Hateg basin wing.

Hatzegopteryx's skull alone was **3 m long**! That is about **one-and-a-half times the length of a bed**.

Hatzegopteryx had **hollow bones** that helped it **fly** and made it very **light**. It probably only **weighed about 250 kg**. That's about the **same as a calf**.

Hatzegopteryx reached the **same height as a giraffe** when walking on land.

It **ate by spearing** its food with its **long beak** in a similar way to a **stork**.

Hatzegopteryx had a **big head** and **strong beak**. It may have **eaten Magyarosaurus** [mod-yar-oh-sore-us], a small sauropod dinosaur.

Hateg Island was cut off from the world so life evolved more slowly. It was home to unusually small animals, such as birds, lizards and even small dinosaurs like Telmatosaurus. Hatzegopteryx was at the **top** of the island **food chain**.

Its wingspan was 10 m wide – that's as wide as an F-16 fighter jet plane.

23

ENORMOUS WINGED QUETZALCOATLUS

One of the most famous pterosaurs is also one of the **biggest flying animals** to have ever lived on Earth. Quetzalcoatlus cast an enormous shadow as it flew through the skies during the **Cretaceous period**.

While Quetzalcoatlus was one of the biggest pterosaurs, it didn't weigh a lot for its size - only **about 250 kg**. Its **bones** were hollow and thin - **as thin as a playing card**. This helped it take to the skies.

Pronounced KET-sal-co-atil-us, **Quetzalcoatlus** is named after the **Aztec feathered serpent god**, Quetzalcoatl, from the area of modern Mexico.

Quetzalcoatlus could snap up small or baby dinosaurs in its huge jaws.

Quetzalcoatlus had a **very long neck** – about **3 m long**. That's **as long as a camel.**

At 2.5 m long, its head was the size of a small car!

This pterosaur had a **bony crest made of keratin,** the same material as your **fingernails.**

Quetzalcoatlus may have used its **long toothless jaw** to **dig for food** in the sand.

Quetzalcoatlus possibly glided rather than flew.

Some scientists suggest it could fly at speeds of **up to 130 kph. That's as fast as a golden eagle.**

This pterosaur's **enormous wingspan** was over **10 m wide**. The bird with the biggest wingspan today is the **wandering albatross.** Its **wingspan is only 3 m across.**

PRETTY PTERODAUSTRO

Pterodaustro was a flying reptile that lived near lakes in what is now **Argentina in South America**. It **hunted** for small crustaceans, such as **shrimp**, as it waded through the shallow waters.

Pterodaustro, pronounced TEH-roe-daws-trow, means southern wing.

A fossilised Pterodaustro **egg** has been **found with the baby** Pterodaustro still **inside**!

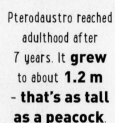

Pterodaustro reached adulthood after 7 years. It **grew** to about **1.2 m** - **that's as tall as a peacock**.

Its **long head and neck** but **short feet** meant it would have needed a long run up to fly, **like a swan** taking off from water today.

Pterodaustro probably **hunted at night**. This would have made it **harder for predators to spot** and there might have been a **greater food supply** when it was dark.

Pterodaustro may have **filtered water in its bill for food**, like **flamingos** today. It might also have been pink!

Its wingspan was about twice the height of you – at 2.5 m wide!

Pterodaustro had about 1,000 teeth in its bill!

Like some dinosaurs, Pterodaustro had **gizzard stones in its stomach**. They may have **helped it digest** its food.

stones

DRESSED TO IMPRESS

What made many pterosaurs stand out from the crowd were their bold and elaborate head crests. Here are some more fancy flying reptiles!

CAIUAJARA

PRONUNCIATION: kai-wua-JAR-a
LENGTH: Unknown
WINGSPAN: 2.3 m
LIVED: Late Cretaceous
LOCATION: Brazil
DIET: Fruit
FACT: Caiuajara had a crest shaped like the sail of a yacht.

TUPANDACTYLUS

PRONUNCIATION: Too-PAN-dak-till-us
LENGTH: Unknown
WINGSPAN: 5 m
LIVED: Cretaceous period
LOCATION: Brazil
DIET: Fish
FACT: Tupandactylus' huge sail-like crest could reach up to a metre in height.

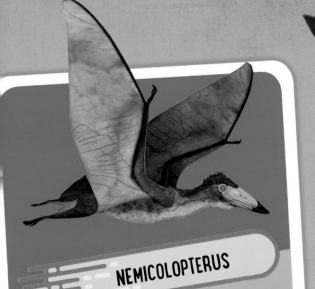

NEMICOLOPTERUS

PRONUNCIATION: neh-mi-COL-opteh-rus
LENGTH: 5 cm
WINGSPAN: 25 cm
LIVED: Cretaceous period
LOCATION: China
DIET: Insects
FACT: Nemicolopterus was the smallest known pterosaur. It was no bigger than a sparrow.

TAPEJARA

PRONUNCIATION: tap-eh-JAR-a
LENGTH: Unknown
WINGSPAN: 3.5 m
LIVED: Cretaceous period
LOCATION: Brazil
DIET: Fish
FACT: Tapejara had an elaborate head crest that was up to a metre tall. It may have used it for mating displays, just like a male peacock uses his tail feathers.

NYCTOSAURUS

PRONUNCIATION: nic-toe-SORE-us
LENGTH: 37 cm
WINGSPAN: At least 2 m
LIVED: Cretaceous period
LOCATION: USA
DIET: Fish
FACT: Nyctosaurus had two long bones sticking out of its head, like deer antlers.

THALASSODROMEUS

PRONUNCIATION: tha-lass-a-DRO-me-us
LENGTH: 1.8 m
WINGSPAN: 4.5-5 m
LIVED: Cretaceous period
LOCATION: Brazil
DIET: Fish and meat
FACT: Thalassodromeus had a crest three times larger than its skull! It is one of the largest pterosaur crests.

GLOSSARY

ammonite an extinct sea creature, often found as a fossil

aquatic relating to water. An aquatic animal is one that lives in water.

Aztecs a group of people who lived in the area of modern Mexico before the 16th century

crest a tuft of feathers, bone, or fur on an animal's head

Cretaceous period a period in Earth's history, between 144 and 65 million years ago

crustacean a group of mostly water creatures with a body made of sections, such as a crab or shrimp

digest the process of breaking down food

dorsal related to the back, as an organ or part of an animal

evolve to develop, change, or improve by steps

expand to make larger

extinct no longer living

filter to pass water through to remove unwanted material

flock a number of birds together

food chain group of living things (animals and plants) where each member of the group is eaten in turn by another

fossil the remains of an animal or plant, preserved for millions of years

gizzard stone a small stone swallowed by some animals to help digestion

Jurassic period a period of Earth's history, between 206 and 144 million years ago

keratin a material that makes up hair, feathers, nails, claws etc.

Loch Ness Monster an aquatic animal that is said to live in the deep waters of Loch Ness in Scotland

Mesozoic Era a period in Earth's history from 251 to 65 million years ago. It is devided into the Triassic, Jurassic and Cretaceous periods.

mollusc an animal that has a soft body and is often covered with a shell, such as a snail

predator an animal that eats other animals

prey an animal that is eaten by other animals

propel to push forward

reptile a cold-blooded animal that breathes air and is often covered with scales

retreat to move back

rudder a piece of wood at the back of the boat that moves from side to side for steering

sauropod a group of dinosaurs that walked on four legs, had long tails and necks, small heads and thick, column-shaped limbs

species a group of closely-related animals that are very similar

Triassic period a period in Earth's history, between 248 and 206 million years ago

wingspan the maximum width of the wings of a flying animal or aircraft

FURTHER INFORMATION

Further Reading

Wild Age: Sea Monsters by Steve Parker (QED Publishing, 2011)

Dangerous Dinosaurs: Flying Monsters by Liz Miles (Franklin Watts, 2015)

Graphic Prehistoric Animals: Mega Shark by Gary Jeffrey (Franklin Watts, 2017)

Sea Monsters: A Prehistoric Adventure by National Geographic Society, (National Geographic Kids 2015)

Websites

www.nhm.ac.uk/discover/mary-anning-unsung-hero.html

www.bbc.co.uk/nature/life/Pterosaur

www.bbc.co.uk/nature/life/Reptile/by/prehistoric

INDEX